# Meditations from Conversations with God

# Meditations from Conversations with God

HAMPTON ROADS
PUBLISHING COMPANY, INC.

NEALE DONALD WALSCH

**Hampton Roads Publishing Company, Inc.**
1125 Stoney Ridge Road
Charlottesville, VA 22902

434-296-2772
Fax: 434-296-5096
E-mail: hrpc@hrpub.com
www.hrpub.com

If you are unable to order this book from your local
bookseller, you may order directly from the publisher.
Call 1-800-766-8009, toll-free.

Library of Congress Cataloging-in-Publication Data available

ISBN 1-57174-513-0

10 9 8 7 6 5 4 3 2 1

This book was conceived, designed, and produced by
**Ixos Press Limited**
The Old Candlemakers, West Street,
Lewes, East Sussex BN7 2NZ, UK
www.ivy-group.co.uk

Publisher: David Alexander
Creative Director: Peter Bridgewater
Art Director: Sarah Howerd
Editorial Director: Caroline Earle
Designer: Simon Goggin
Picture Researchers: Katie Greenwood, Shelley Noronha

Printed in China

# Contents

# Introduction

In February 1992 Neale Donald Walsch had an experience that was to change not only his life, but the lives of millions of people around the globe. This was the month in which God began to speak to him and in fact entered into a rather extensive dialogue with him. These exchanges were eventually to become a book, *Conversations with God*, which was an international bestseller read by millions of people in dozens of languages around the world. This book spawned two highly successful sequels in the *Conversations with God* trilogy.

For Neale, these conversations quenched an enormous thirst and satisfied an incredible hunger. Readers everywhere have been similarly touched and have attested to the comfort and guidance they have found in the pages of these books.

Like many of us, Neale had been searching for the God of his heart for a very long time. The God he met in his conversations turned out to be not a God of fear, but a God of unconditional and

unlimited love. A God of deep compassion and understanding. A God of wonderful humor. A God who takes pure delight in the joyful celebration of life. He met a God who offers friendship, not lordship—and who in return asks for friendship, not worship.

The meditations included in this book are derived from Neale's dialogues with God. They address issues many of us confront in our daily lives, and some that we will all face at some point. The depth of their universal wisdom shines through and all who have been involved in the making of this book have been deeply affected and have found great comfort and guidance, as we feel sure that you, the reader, will too.

You may wish to read this book from cover to cover or simply to dip into from time to time when you are seeking comfort or advice. Or, if you a particular issue is on your mind, use the index at the back of the book for guidance. This is a book that you will come back to time and time again.

# Meditations on
# Universal Truths

# On creating reality

You do not live each day to *discover* what it holds for you, but to *create* it. You are creating your reality every minute, probably without knowing it.

# On coming to terms with your Self

There comes a time in the evolution of every soul when the chief concern is no longer the survival of the physical body, but the growth of the spirit; no longer the attainment of worldly success, but the realization of Self.

# On bad people

I am going to tell you this: there are no "rotten apples."
There are only people who disagree with your point of
view on things, people who construct a different model
of the world. I am going to tell you this: no persons do
anything inappropriate, given their model of the world.

# On power

*Power comes from inner strength. Inner strength does not come from raw power.* In this, most of the world has it backwards.

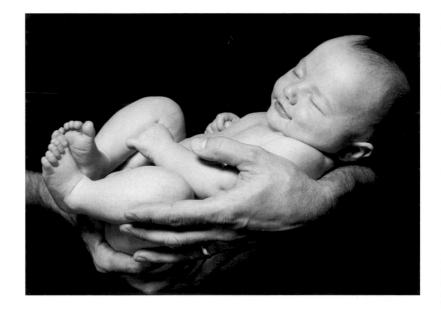

# On who you are

Everything that occurs—everything that has occurred, is occurring, and ever will occur—is the outward physical manifestation of your innermost thoughts, choices, ideas, and determination regarding Who You Are and Who You Choose to Be.

# On the one reality

Yes, there is One Great Truth; there is a Final Reality.
But you will always get what you choose, regardless
of that reality—precisely because the reality is that you
are a divine creature, divinely creating your reality even
as you are experiencing it.

# On the forgiveness
# of sins

In truth, I do *not* forgive you, and will not forgive you *ever*,
for *anything*. I do not have to. There is nothing to forgive.
But I can release you. And I hereby do. Now. Once again.
As I have done so often in the past, through the teachings
of so many other teachers.

# Meditations on
# The Spiritual Path

# On religion and spirituality

Religion cannot stand Spirituality. It cannot abide it. For
Spirituality may bring you to a different conclusion than a
particular religion—and this no known religion can tolerate.

Religion encourages you to explore the thoughts of
others and accept them as your own. Spirituality invites
you to toss away the thoughts of others and come
up with your own.

# On God

I tell you, I am in every flower, every rainbow, every
star in the heavens, and everything in and on every
planet rotating around every star.

I am the whisper of the wind, the warmth of your
sun, the incredible individuality and the extraordinary
perfection of every snowflake.

I am the majesty in the soaring flight of eagles,
and the innocence of the doe in the field; the
courage of lions, the wisdom of the ancient ones.

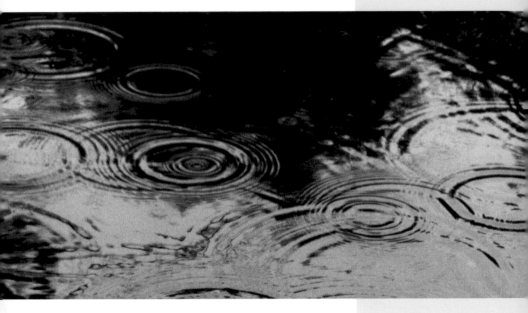

# On holiness

Every day is sanctified. Every *minute* is holy.
*This*, *now*, is the *Holy Instant*.

# On the fulfillment of your Divine Self

Do not waste the precious moments of this, your present reality, seeking to unveil all of life's secrets.

Those secrets are secret for a reason. Grant your God the benefit of the doubt. Use your Now Moment for the Highest Purpose—the creation and the expression of Who You Really Are.

*Decide* Who You Are—Who you *want* to be—and then do everything in your power to *be* that.

# On expressing your Divine Connection with the All

Embrace every circumstance, own every fault, share every joy, contemplate every mystery, walk in every man's shoes, forgive every offense (including your own), heal every heart, honor every person's truth, adore every person's God, protect every person's rights, preserve every person's dignity, promote every person's interests, provide every person's needs, presume every person's holiness, present every person's greatest gifts, produce every person's blessing, and pronounce every person's future secure in the assured love of God.

# On making the right decisions

If all you desired is what your soul desired, everything
would be very simple. If you listened to the part of you
which is pure spirit, all of your decisions would be easy,
and all the outcomes joyous.

# Meditations
# on Feelings

# On truth

Feelings are neither negative nor destructive.
They are simply truths. How you express your
truth is what matters.

# On expressing your feelings

It is not nearly so important how well a message is received as how well it is sent.

You cannot take responsibility for how well another accepts your truth; you can only ensure how well it is communicated. And by how well, I don't mean merely how clearly; I mean how lovingly, how compassionately, how sensitively, how courageously, and how completely.

# On understanding your true feelings

Feelings *are* the language of the soul, but you must make sure you are listening to your *true feelings* and not some counterfeit model constructed in your mind.

# On hurting others

If acting irresponsibly, if behaving in a way which
you know might damage others or cause hardship
or pain, is what makes you "feel good," then you
have not evolved very far.

# On fear and guilt

Guilt is a blight upon the land—the poison that kills
the plant.

You will not grow through guilt, but only shrivel and die.

Awareness is what you seek. But awareness is not guilt,
and love is not fear.

Fear and guilt...are your only enemies. Love and
awareness are your true friends. Yet do not confuse the
one with the other, for one will kill you, while the other
gives you life.

# On love and fear

Ultimately, all thoughts are sponsored by love or fear.
This is the great polarity. This is the primal duality.
Everything, ultimately, breaks down to one of these.
All thoughts, ideas, concepts, understandings, decisions,
choices, and actions are based in one of these.

And, in the end, there is really only one.

Love.

In truth, love is all there is. Even fear is an outgrowth
of love and, when used effectively, expresses love.

# On grief

Grief is a natural emotion. It's the part of you which allows
you to say goodbye when you don't want to say goodbye;
to express—push out, propel—the sadness within you at
the experience of any kind of loss.

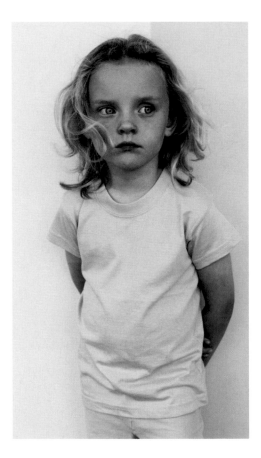

# On anger

Anger is a natural emotion. It is the tool you have which allows you to say, "No, thank you." It does not have to be abusive, and it never has to be damaging to another.

# On envy

Envy is the natural emotion that makes you want to do it
again; to try harder; to continue striving until you succeed.

# On fear

The purpose of natural fear is to build in a bit of caution.
Caution is a tool that helps keep the body alive.

# Meditations on Mortality

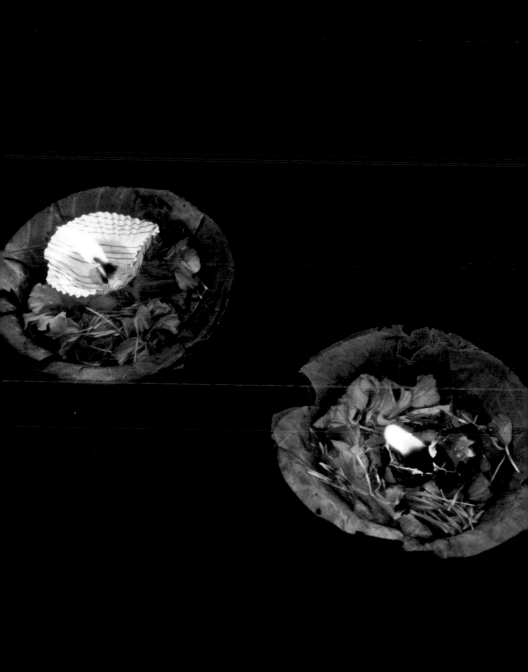

# On personal evolution

The soul is very clear that its purpose is evolution…it
is not concerned with the achievements of the body or
the development of the mind. These are all meaningless
to the soul.

The soul is also very clear that there is no great tragedy
involved in leaving the body. In many ways the tragedy
is being *in* the body.

# On the fear of dying

You think that life on Earth is better than life in heaven?
I tell you this, at the moment of your death you will realize
the greatest freedom, the greatest peace, the greatest joy,
and the greatest love you have ever known.

# On transforming yourself

Even the rock will not be a rock forever, but only what "seems like forever." Before it was a rock, it was something else. It fossilized into that rock, through a process taking hundreds of thousands of years. It was once something else, and will be something else again.

# On understanding death

First, understand that death is not an end, but a beginning;
not a horror, but a joy. It is not a closing down, but an
opening up.

The happiest moment in your life will be the moment
it ends.

That's because it *doesn't* end but only goes on in ways
so magnificent, so full of peace and wisdom and joy,
as to make it difficult to describe and impossible for
you to comprehend.

# On the illusion of death

See the flower as dying and you will see the flower sadly.
Yet see the flower as part of a whole tree that is changing,
and will soon bear fruit, and you see the flower's true
beauty. When you understand that the blossoming and
the falling away of the flower is a sign that the tree is
ready to bear fruit, then you understand life.

Look at this carefully, and you will see that life is its
own metaphor.

# Meditations on
# Self-Awareness

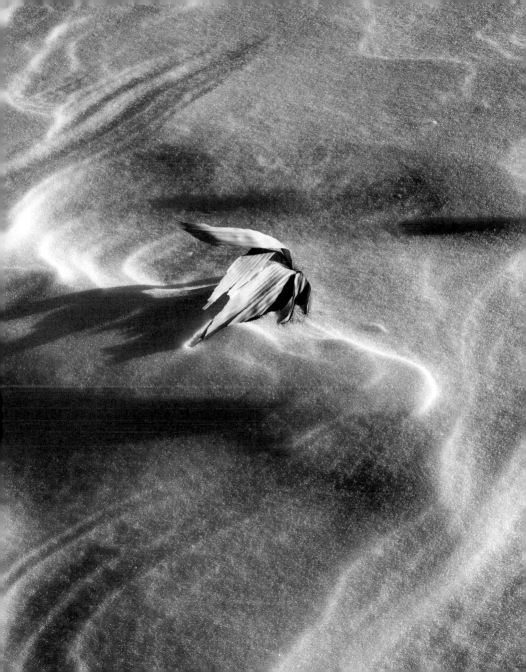

# On living on a higher plane

Go to your Highest Thought about yourself. Imagine the
you that you would be if you lived that thought every day.
Imagine what you would think, do, and say, and how you
would respond to what others do and say.

Do you see any difference between that projection
and what you think, do, and say now?

# On creating yourself

Remember, you are constantly in the act of creating
yourself. You are in every moment deciding who and what
you are. You decide this largely through the choices you
make regarding who and what you feel passionate about.

# On passion

Passion is the love of turning being into action. It fuels
the engine of creation. It changes concepts to experience.
…Never deny passion, for that is to deny Who You Are,
and Who You Truly Want to Be.

# On self-esteem

A tree is no less perfect because it is a seedling. A tiny
infant is no less perfect than a grown-up. It is *perfection
itself*. Because it cannot *do* a thing, does not *know* a thing,
that does not make it somehow less perfect.

A child makes mistakes. She stands. She toddles.
She falls. She stands again, a bit wobbly, hanging on to
her mommy's leg. Does that make the child imperfect?

I tell you it is just the opposite! That child is *perfection
itself*, wholly and completely adorable.

So, too, are *you*.

# On being a bringer
# of the light

Be a Bringer of the Light. For your light can do more than
illuminate your own path. Your light can be the light
which truly lights the world.

# On not being affected by what others say

People can relate to you—even as they judge you. And if they see that you are truly sincere, they can even forgive you your "sordid past."

Yet I tell you this: So long as you are still worried about what others think of you, you are owned by them.

Only when you require no approval from outside yourself can you own yourself.

# Meditations
## on Time

# On spending your time wisely

When you spend your time trying to figure out what's "best" for you, you are doing just that: *spending your time*. Better to save your time than to spend it wastefully.

# On throwing caution to the wind

If you spend your time trying to figure out what's "best" for you, your choices will be cautious, your decisions will take forever, and your journey will be launched on a sea of expectations.

If you are not careful, you will *drown* in your expectations.

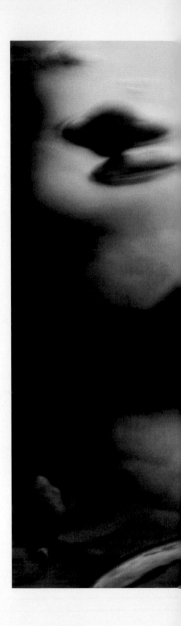

# On recognizing the importance of the moment

There is no time like the present! You've heard that before, I'm sure...

There is no time but *this* time. There is no moment but this moment. "Now" is all there is...

"Yesterday" and "tomorrow" are figments of your imagination. Constructions of your mind. Nonexistent in Ultimate Reality.

Everything that ever happened, is happening, and ever will happen, is happening right *now*.

# On the passage of time

Past, present, and future are concepts you have constructed, realities you have invented, in order to create a context within which to frame your present experience.

# On the decisions
# you make today

Remember, life is an ongoing process of creation.
You are creating your reality every minute.
The decision you make today is often not the choice
you make tomorrow. Yet here is a secret of all Masters:
*keep choosing the same thing*.

# On the here and now

Ignore your previous experience and *go into the moment*.
Be Here Now.

# Meditations on
# Politics and War

# On the folly of not following your own instincts

In most cases you've chosen to accept someone else's decision. Someone who came before you and, presumably, knows better... This is especially true on important matters. In fact, the more important the matter, the less likely you are to listen to your own experience, and the more ready you seem to be to make someone else's ideas your own.

# On tolerating war

Most people are satisfied with a world in which differences, not similarities, are honored, and disagreements are settled by conflict and war.

# On maintaining
# the status quo

Most people *laugh* when one suggests any kind of system
other than the one currently in place, saying that behaviors
such as competing and killing and the "victor taking the
spoils" are what makes civilization *great*!

# On changing by example

Consciousness is everything, and creates your experience. *Group* consciousness is powerful and produces outcomes of unspeakable beauty or ugliness. The choice is always yours.

If you are not satisfied with the consciousness of your group, seek to change it.

The best way to change the consciousness of others is by your example.

# On the justification of foreign policy decisions

It is not wrong to base foreign policy decisions on vested interest considerations. What is wrong is to pretend that you're not doing so.

This most countries do, of course. They take action—or *fail* to take action—for one set of reasons, then give as a rationale another set of reasons.

# On the deception
# of governments

There are very few governments which do not deliberately
mislead their people. Deception is part of government,
for few people would choose to be governed the way
they are governed—few would choose to be governed
at all—unless government convinced them that its
decisions were for their own good.

# Meditations
## on **Money**

# On what you do for a living

If you think your life is about doingness, you do not understand what you are about. Your soul doesn't care *what* you do for a living—and when your life is over, neither will you. Your soul cares only about what you're *being* while you're doing *whatever* you're doing. It is a state of beingness the soul is after, not a state of doingness.

# On hunger, thirst, and shelter

Take the $1,000,000,000,000 spent annually worldwide for military purposes and shift that to humanitarian purposes, and you will have solved the problem [of world hunger, thirst, and shelter] without spending an additional penny or shifting *any* of the wealth from where it now resides to where it does not.

# On possessions

There's nothing I have to have, there's nothing I have
to do, and there's nothing I have to be, except exactly
what I'm being right now.

# On economic versus humanitarian interests

The struggle between the "haves" and the "have-nots" has been going on forever and is epidemic on your planet. It will ever be thus so long as economic interests, rather than humanitarian interests, run the world—so long as man's body, and not man's soul, is man's highest concern.

# Meditations
## on The Planet

# On God's universal presence

I am the wind which rustles your hair. I am the sun which warms your body. I am the rain which dances on your face. I am the smell of the flowers in the air, and I am the flowers which send their fragrance upward. I am the air which *carries* the fragrance.

# On destruction
# of the planet

Most people do not see that they are destroying
their Earth—the very planet which gives them
*Life*—because their actions seek only to enhance
their quality of life.

# On the cycle of life

Understanding about the life of the universe will help
you to understand about the life of the universe inside *you*.

Life moves in cycles. Everything is cyclical. Everything.
When you understand this, you become more able to
enjoy the Process—not merely endure it.

All things move cyclically. There is a natural rhythm to
life, and everything moves to that rhythm; everything goes
with that flow. Thus it is written: "For everything there is
a season; and a time for every Purpose under Heaven."

# On the wisdom
# of women

A woman hears the melody of flowers in the wind. She
sees the beauty of the Unseen. She feels the tugs and
pulls and urges of life. She *knows* when it is time to run,
and time to rest; time to laugh and time to cry; time to
hold on and time to let go.

# On living in harmony

This is the great secret. This is the sacred wisdom.
*Do unto others as you would have it done unto you.*

All of your problems, all of your conflicts, all of your
difficulties in creating a life on your planet of peace and
joy are based in your failure to understand this simple
instruction, and to follow it.

# On there being no separation

Act as if you were separate from nothing, and no one,
and you will heal your world tomorrow.

This is the greatest secret of all time.

# Meditations
## on Relationships

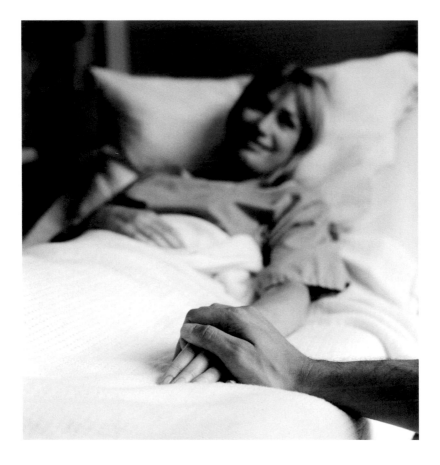

# On marriage

This is a day-to-day, hour-to-hour, moment-to-moment act of supreme consciousness. It is a choosing and a re-choosing every instant. It is ongoing creation...using the tools of creation... and using them with awareness and sublime intention.

# On understanding what makes relationships work

Most people enter relationships with an eye toward what they can get out of them, rather than what they can put into them. The purpose of relationship is to decide what part of yourself you'd like to see "show up," not what part of another you can capture and hold.

# On acting in an ungodly way

If you have caught yourself in an ungodly act as a result of doing what is best for you, the confusion is not in having put yourself first, but rather in misunderstanding what is best for you.

# On acting naturally

If you act lovingly, you will be acting naturally. If you react
fearfully, resentfully, angrily, you may be acting *normally*,
but you will never be acting *naturally*.

# On parenting

Most parents come to the job of parenting with very little life experience. They're hardly finished being parented themselves. They're still looking for answers, still searching for clues.

# On the wisdom
# of the elders

It is the elders who know of truth, and life. Of what is
important and what is not. Of what is really meant by such
terms as integrity, honesty, loyalty, friendship, and love.

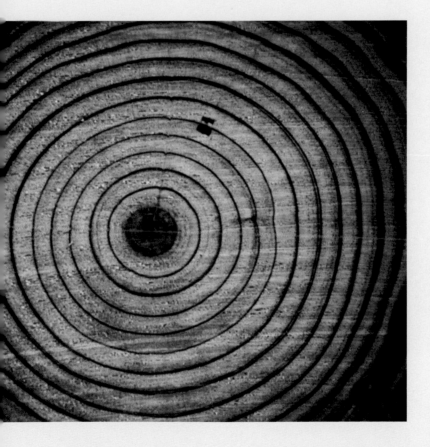

# On your duty to others

Let this be your task, let this be your greatest joy: to give people back to themselves. Even in their darkest hour. Especially in that hour.

# On considering how you are acting

Let each person in the relationship worry not about the other, but only, only, only about the *Self*...the most loving person is the person who is Self-centered.

# Index

# Acknowledgments

The publisher would like to thank the following organizations for the use of images in this book.
Every effort has been made to acknowledge the pictures, however we apologize if there are any unintentional omissions.

**Corbis**: 15 (Terry W. Eggers), 19 (Miles/Zefa), 25 (Peter Adams/Zefa), 29 (B. Bird/Zefa), 36 (Tony Demin),
49 (Take 2 Productions/Ken Kaminesky), 51 (SIE Productions/Zefa), 55 (Janez Skok), 56 (Grace/Zefa), 60 (Mark A. Johnson),
63 (Anders Ryman), 65 (Chris Rainier), 71 (Theo Allofs/Zefa), 80 (Stacy Morrison/Zefa), 89 (Frank Krahmer/Zefa),
91 (Blasius Erlinger/Zefa), 96 (Blasius Erlinger/Zefa), 100 (Guntmar Fritz/Zefa), 103 (Frank Krahmer/Zefa), 106 (Richard T. Nowitz),
109 (Photex/Photex/Zefa), 111 (Bettmann), 121 (Frans Lemmens/Zefa), 127 (Paul Edmondson), 145 (PBNJ Productions),
147 (Chris Rainier), 149 (LWA-Dann Tardif/Zefa), 157 (Louis Moses/Zefa).

**Getty Images**: 20 (PM Images/Stone+), 35, 41(Nevada Wier/The Image Bank), 43 (Art Wolfe/Stone+), 45 (Ilja Herb/Aurora),
46 (Masaaki Toyoura/Taxi), 52 (Aaron McCoy/Taxi), 59 (Laurence Dutton/The Image Bank), 79 (Kieran Scott/Stone+),
86 (Johner/ Johner Images), 93 (Richard Seagraves/Workbook Stock), 99 (Petrified Collection/Image Bank),
112 (White Packert/Iconica),117 (Glen Allison/Stone), 122 (Camille Tokerud/Photographer's Choice),
125 (Leo Pavelle/Hulton Archive), 135 (ML Harris/Iconica), 141 (Michael Kelley/Stone+),142 (VCL/Alistair Berg/Taxi),
149 (Michael Edwards/Stone), 153 (Jochem D Wijnands/The Image Bank), 154 (Steve Casimiro/Photographer's Choice).

**Osho International Foundation**: 83.

---

Hampton Roads Publishing Company publishes books on a variety of subjects,
including metaphysics, spirituality, health, visionary fiction, and other related topics.

We also create on-line courses and sponsor author workshops.
For a current list of what is available, go to www.hrpub.com,
or e-mail us at hrpc@hrpub.com.

For a copy of our latest trade catalog,
call toll-free, 800-766-8009,
or send your name and address to:

Hampton Roads Publishing Company, Inc.
1125 Stoney Ridge Road
Charlottesville, VA 22902
E-mail: hrpc@hrpub.com
Internet: www.hrpub.com